IMAGES OF ENGLAND

SHEFFIELD INDUSTRIES

CUTLERY, SILVER AND EDGE TOOLS

The Year Knife. This complex and wonderful knife was made in 1821, and reputedly has a blade for each year of the Christian era. A new blade was apparently added for every year and in the year 2000 the knife will be complete. It is in the shape of a star, which is part of Joseph Rodgers' trademark.

IMAGES OF ENGLAND

SHEFFIELD INDUSTRIES
CUTLERY, SILVER AND EDGE TOOLS

JOAN UNWIN AND KEN HAWLEY

The History Press

First published 1999
Reprinted 2002, 2005

Reprinted in 2013 by
The History Press
The Mill, Brimscombe Port,
Stroud, Gloucestershire, GL5 2QG
www.thehistorypress.co.uk

British Library Cataloguing in Publication Data.
A catalogue record for this book is available from the British Library.

ISBN 978 0 7524 1658 8

Typesetting and origination by Tempus Publishing Limited.
Printed in Great Britain.

Contents

Acknowledgements

The authors would like to thank the Ken Hawley Collection Trust for permission to use the photographs in the Collection and the University of Sheffield for their support in housing and staffing the Collection.

Our thanks to the following people and companies who have helped us and who have given permission for the use of material: Mr Brian Alcock; Aurora Metals Ltd – Hot Rolled Products (formerly Spencer Clark Ltd); Mrs Christine Ball; Dr Simon Barley; British Silverware; Mrs Elizabeth Crossley; Egginton Group of Companies; Firth Rixson; Footprint Tools; Gemeentearchif Amsterdam; Harrison Fisher; Mappin & Webb Ltd; Mr Harry Melling; Miss Margaret Oversby; Mr Peter Perry; Edward Pryor & Son Ltd; Mr Gordon Ragg; Record Tools Ltd; Mr Laurence Richardson; Sheffield Newspapers Ltd; Mr Dennis Smith; Mr Wallace Smyth; Spear and Jackson; Stanley Tools (UK) Ltd; Swann-Morton Ltd; Timken Latrobe Steel – Europe Ltd; Mr Colin Turner; Mr Basil Walker; Worldwide Photography Ltd; Mrs Wragg.

Every attempt has been made to trace the original owners of the photographs used in this publication, but changes in company ownership, etc., have meant that some people may have been missed. For this we apologise.

Introduction

This collection of photographs is a homage to Sheffield craftsmen. Sheffield has a long tradition of metalworking – cutlery, steel-making, the manufacture of tools and later silver manufacture. Documentary evidence for knife-making goes back to 1297, when Robert the Cutler was listed in a tax return. Cutlers made up a substantial proportion of the workforce in the later Middle Ages and by Elizabethan times the trade was controlled by the Lords of the Manor of Hallamshire – the Earls of Shrewsbury. In 1624, following the death of the last Earl, the cutlers of Sheffield applied for an Act of Parliament which incorporated the Company of Cutlers in Hallamshire. This body then controlled all aspects of the trades of knife, scissor, sickle and shear manufacture. At the end of the seventeenth century the craftsmen making scythes, awl blades and files joined the Company.

The location of Sheffield was an advantage in the development of metalworking trades. Local ironstone was exploited in the Middle Ages and later, when the skills base was well established, iron and steel were imported through eastern coastal ports. The fast-flowing rivers from the west provided power for the forges and grinding wheels. Until the nineteenth century, most knife and tool manufacturing processes could be carried out in small workshops and with a few simple tools.

In the nineteenth century, with the introduction of steam power, large factories were built which generally consisted of numbers of individual workshops. Large factories built for one manufacturer only were rare. The traditional manufacturing organisation of the 'Little Mester' in his workshop – the individual craftsman with perhaps two or three employees and apprentices – continued alongside the increasing number of factories with production-line processes. Only gradually did the more well-known names appear with large integrated factories – cutlers like Joseph Rodgers, silver manufacturers like James Dixon and toolmakers such as Ward and Payne.

Edge tools – chisels, saws, spades, shovels etc. – have been made in Sheffield since at least the mid-eighteenth century, although there is surprisingly little documentary evidence about the early manufacturers. Many of the processes are similar to cutlery manufacture and undoubtedly the skills were transferable. Technological advances, such as the invention of crucible steel, the improved ability to roll steel sheets and bars and finally, in the nineteenth century, bulk production of steel, all aided the increased production of edge tools. Many of the tool manufacturers worked in small factories, few developing into the size of the biggest cutlery firms.

Silver manufacture in Sheffield greatly expanded after the invention of Sheffield Plate in the mid-eighteenth century. The fusion of silver onto copper allowed many costly silver articles – trays, teapots and candlesticks – to be made more cheaply. The improved steel created by the crucible method allowed high quality dies to be used and stamped-out spoons, candlesticks and trays were produced by the thousand. Silver plate accounted for most of the output – firstly as Sheffield Plate, then, from around 1840, as electroplate on nickel silver. Although the industry made use of heavy stamps and presses for many of its manufacturing processes, handmade articles formed a large proportion of output.

This collection of photographs comes principally from the Hawley Tool Collection. Many of the photographs have been donated by craftsmen and firms, some have been taken by the collector Ken Hawley and others are reprints of illustrations from old trade catalogues or company histories. Taking photographs of people at work was not a very common occurrence. Often, photographs were taken because the craftsman was one of the last, or because the factory was about to close, and so represent a glimpse of bygone working methods. Several firms, on the building of new factories, would proudly commission photographs for their catalogues, firm's history or publicity material. Generally, however, Sheffielders have been rather shy about having their photograph taken doing what they consider to be 'nothing special'. It is only through these photographs that the majority of people can appreciate their skills, most of which have now disappeared.

The book is divided into three sections – cutlery, edge tools and silver – and includes a glossary of terms at the end.

One

Cutlery

In Sheffield terms, cutlery is 'that what cuts', i.e. knives (table knives, spring knives and trade knives), scissors and razors. Spoons and forks are 'flatware', while dishes, bowls and teapots, etc. are 'hollow-ware'. There are three main processes in cutlery manufacture. Firstly, the blade is made. Originally, this was hand-forged from bars of steel, or of iron with a thin strip of steel for the edge. Forges were small buildings, with a smithy hearth for reheating the metal and an anvil or stiddy for hammering out the blade. Today, most blades are stamped out of sheet steel using large presses.

The second process is to grind and glaze the knife blade, which at the same time puts a cutting edge on it. Power was supplied either by a foot treadle or by hand, but by the eighteenth century water power was the norm. Natural sandstone was once used to make grinding wheels, but the dust created during grinding caused the deadly disease of silicosis. The grinding wheel rotated in a trough of water and the grinder sat astride the 'horsin' seat, with the wheel rotating away from him. Water-powered grinding hulls were built on all of Sheffield's rivers. The drive belts ran to each 'trow' with its wheel and these were rented out to grinders. Later, steam power was used, then electric motors, and the natural sandstones were replaced by man-made, composite abrasive wheels. Grinding machines, taking many blades at a time, are now used.

The final stage of manufacture is to attach a handle, polish the knife and pack it up for dispatch. The supply of materials for handles was another huge trade in Sheffield, with the import of natural items such as horn, ivory, shell, pearl and exotic woods. In the late nineteenth century plastics, such as xylonite, were introduced and natural handle materials are now rarely used.

John Wilson, cutlery manufacturers. This title page from the 1937 catalogue, showing hundreds of varieties of butchers' knives, gives an indication of the vast range of tradesmen's knives made in Sheffield up to the Second World War. Enormous quantities were exported to the meat packing stations in Argentina, Australia, South Africa and elsewhere. Food preparation trades dealing with cattle, pigs, fish, butter and cheese all had their specific knives. There was an almost endless list of specialist trades, such as shoe, basket and saddlery manufacture, as well as tradesmen in the painting, plumbing and confectionery trades, who also had their own knives.

Examples of knives spanning approximately 700 years. From left to right: leaf-bladed knife, 13th century; knife with struck mark, 14th/15th century; with inlaid mark, 14th/15th century; with inlaid mark, 16th century; with mark of B and fishhook, registered by Richard Bocking in 1685; with carved ivory handle, late 18th century; early stainless steel blade, 1920s; knife with hollow metal handle, 1960s; solid metal knife, 1960s.

This unusual cutlery was designed in the early 1930s to be produced from flat sheet steel, requiring no separate blade-forging and handle-fitting. The designer was Douglas Clark, of the firm of George Clark, North British Steel Works, Sheffield. The firm rolled steel into sheet form for the shovel, spade and saw industries. The design was an attempt to break into the cutlery market but was unsuccessful as the knives were not well balanced.

For many years now, the Stanley knife has replaced the traditional pocket knife. It was invented in the USA factory in 1935 for cutting the new material – softboard. A price list of July 1949 for Stanley (Sheffield) includes the knives, which were being imported. The Stanley knife began to be manufactured here in the 1960s and currently some three million blades a week are being produced.

Albert Craven, pen and pocket blade forger, 1960s. Albert's hearth and workshop was in a little complex of buildings on Broomspring Lane, typical of Sheffield's small workshops. He holds the forged blade in tongs, with the forging hammer in his right hand.

William Truelove of Crabtree Works, Annesley Road, Greenhill, 1950s. William is forging tea pruner blades. The steel bar already has one forged blade at the end by his hand. When he has finished, both blades will be cut off and the blades heated for a second time to draw out the tang. After grinding and glazing the blade, beechwood 'scales' will then be pinned onto the tang to form the handle. It is thought that no one now does this class of work in the UK.

George Butler, cutlery manufacturer. This wonderful action photograph from the 1920s catalogue shows how the bolster on a hand-forged carving knife was formed. Previously, the shear steel blade would have been 'shut' or forged onto a wrought-iron bar, which would form the bolster and the tang. On the anvil is a pair of top and bottom 'prints' or dies. The hot iron was placed in the dies and struck with a 14lb striking hammer to form the shape of the bolster. On the shelf behind the forger are a variety of bolster prints.

Upper Cut and Nether Cut Wheels, Rivelin Valley, early twentieth century. One of the reasons for the rapid development of Sheffield's cutlery and tool industries was the availability of water for power. Sheffield had five fast-flowing rivers and more streams in adjacent villages, such as Eckington. Water power was used to drive cutlery grinding wheels, forges and rolling mills, as well as for making paper, grinding corn or snuff and polishing glass. These two eighteenth-century wheels were for cutlery grinding and were in use until the early years of the twentieth century.

Grinding a butcher blade, Garden Street, late 1970s. This was heavy work. In order to press the blade against the wheel, a piece of wood called a 'flatstick' was used. This enabled the grinder to grip the blade and control the grinding process. He watched the stream of sparks to see where the blade was being ground, even though the blade was out of sight under the flatstick. Note that he is standing in order to let his weight do the work.

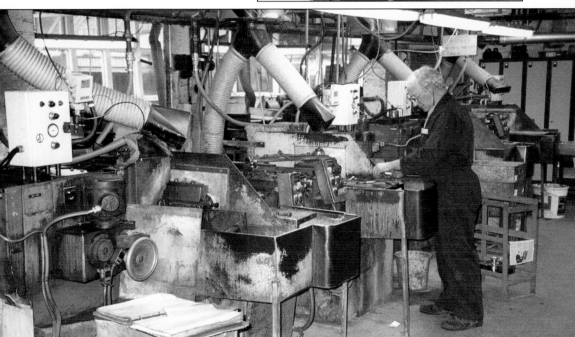

A blade-grinding machine at Harrison Fisher's Eye Witness Works, 1999. Engineer Horace Cowlishaw uses a micrometer to set the Berger AS1 grinding machine. The extractor fans are in evidence.

Mr Lindley, a grinder in Solly Street, 1970s, using the pole method of grinding. The pole is a piece of wood, about 2in square and 3ft long, with an old nail stuck into the end. The nail is pushed into the splat board, in front of the wheel, so forming a lever. The article to be ground is then placed between the pole and the wheel and, if required, enormous pressure can be applied without too much effort from the grinder. The grinder here has the pole end in his left hand and the handle of the article being ground in his right hand.

Brian Alcock, grinder, 1985. Palette knife grinding requires great skill and judgement to achieve the required flexibility without making the blade too thin. Brian is grinding a palette knife using a 'flatstick', which enables him to apply the necessary pressure to the flexible blade when grinding up to the bolster.

A butcher knife cutler and his lad, 1930s, boring scales and pinning them onto a knife tang. This is a scene that must have been enacted countless times in Sheffield workshops. In the late twentieth century, health and safety requirements mean that most knife handles are made from plastic materials, moulded on to the blade.

George Butler, cutlery manufacturer, 1920s. In the foreground, the seated cutler is boring a hole into an ivory table knife handle, which will take the tang. This was done with a parser, a square steel rod with a filed point and a bobbin on the other end to take the drive belt. The parser was fitted into two brackets screwed to the bench. The knife handle was held in the left hand of the cutler and pressure exerted by his left leg. Every quarter-inch or so, the handle was turned through 180° to counteract any tendency to drill off the centre line through the handle. The hole could be as long as five inches but mistakes were very rare indeed.

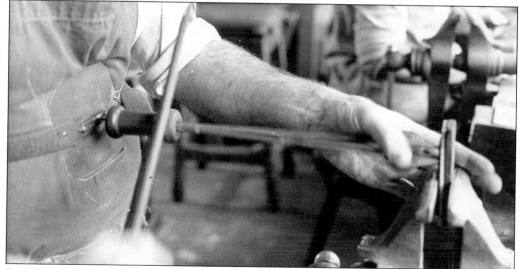

Eric Wragg, spring knife cutler, 1980s. It was the Sheffield cutlers' proud boast that they could bore a hole of any shape. The cutler used a two-legged parser which was rotated by a 'fiddle stick' with a leather thong. A hardened steel template was held against the item to be bored and the two legs of the parser inserted. As the parser rotated, the legs moved round the inside of the template, however complicated the shape. The depth of cut could be regulated by the length of the cutting edge at the end of the parser legs.

Eric Wragg, spring knife cutler, 1980s. Eric is finishing off a pruning knife on a polishing head. The traditional way of making knives required that all the parts had to be ground and filed by hand. This was because all the components were hand-forged and hand-ground and the knife coverings were natural materials, usually from animals – pearl, buffalo horn, stag and ivory. Very few trades survived for so long working in this manner. Not surprisingly, such work practices have almost disappeared.

George Wostenholm, cutlery manufacturers. The impressive Washington Works of George Wostenholm, cutlery manufacturers, was bombed during the Second World War and was partly rebuilt to a more modern plan. Here, in the 1950s, glazers and polishers are at work putting a final finish on the blades of trade knives. Note how the work is carried from one place to another on 'workboards', of which every Sheffield trade had its own variation.

Hill Brothers, Horn Handle Works, 1970s. An important Sheffield trade was horn handle making, which sometimes went alongside ivory cutting and carving. Natural materials – horn, ivory, stag and wood – were used to make the handles for all types of cutlery, as well as for walking sticks and umbrellas. Hill Brothers was one of many firms supplying finished and part-finished material.

The interior of Hill Brothers, just after closure in the late 1970s, shows the cluttered bench with the belt-driven lathes for turning horn. Celluloid, an early plastic, was extremely flammable and the heat generated in sawing pieces could ignite dust and cause a fire. Many old kitchen knives had burnt handles when people forgot about this characteristic. To prevent such accidents in the factory, the circular saw on the right is running in a trough of water. By the 1960s most handles were made of plastic and the trade in natural handles declined.

Ivory and stag stores, Joseph Rodgers, cutlery manufacturer, *c.* 1912. For centuries ivory has been used in Sheffield for knife handles. Its importance is demonstrated by the fact that the coat of arms of the Cutlers' Company, incorporated in 1624, shows an elephant's head. Although the use of ivory and tortoiseshell is now banned, they did provide beautiful handles, being used only on cutlery for the top end of the market. The stag store shows the quantity and variety of horn which had been imported from around the world. The horn was used to make the handles for table knives, razors, pen knives and pocket knives.

Billy Hukin, Sheffield's last razor grinder, 1970s. Here he is hollow grinding a razor at J. & W. Ragg's Little London Works. Two four-inch-diameter grinding wheels rotate towards each other, one fixed, while the other has sideways movement controlled by a lever on the left hand side. A work rest between the wheels supports the blade, which is moved in and out by Billy's right hand. When enough material has been removed, the blade then goes through thirty-six more grinding and polishing processes before the open razor blade is completed.

Razor grinders at John Clarke & Son Ltd, Cutlers, Mowbray Street, c. 1920. Sixty-five years later, Billy Hukin was able to identify several of these. On the left is Ernest Ludlam, the other

two men being the Burkinshaw brothers. The belt in the foreground is off the pulley, revealing the buckle belt fastener.

Razor grinders' workshop at C. Myers, Athol Road, *c.* 1940. This is a view of the workshop where the glazing and polishing processes were performed. Near the stairs is the large electric motor that drove all the workshop's machinery by means of belts and shafting. The room looks far too clean and tidy for a Sheffield workshop, which was usually full of clutter.

Billy Hukin, razor grinder (right). Billy was, by choice, still working in his mid-seventies. He always walked to and from work up quite a steep hill, including returning home for lunch. On the left is Tom Renshaw, a razor 'setter-in', who sets the blade into the scales. This photograph was taken at J & W Ragg's Little London Works in the 1970s. Raggs were the last razor manufacturers in Sheffield, finishing making razors in 1977, but Billy kept on working.

Billy Hukin examining a razor to see how much more grinding it would require. One test for checking the thickness of the blade was to press the edge against the thumbnail. This bent the blade slightly and a knowledgeable eye could determine whether more grinding was needed.

The office of John Clarke & Son Ltd, 1920s. The typist sits at a high desk, more usually associated with writing in heavy ledgers.

John Clarke & Son Ltd, 1920s. The showroom was quite a humble affair, with a selection of cutlery on cards and in boxes. Note the memorial on the wall for the employees who died in the First World War.

Scissor grinding at a workshop in Arundel Street, 1970s. The blade had to be ground on both sides as well as the back edge. Scissor blades are not flat ground, but have a 'set' – a slight curve to make the blades pass each other properly when in use.

Scissor shank dressing, Arundel Street, 1970s. The shanks on a pair of scissors join the blades to the bows where the fingers fit. The rough forgings have to be ground smooth.

Scissors consist of two blades, held together with a screw or rivet so that they cut cleanly and sweetly. The blade points must just touch and the blades must cut along their whole length. This final assembly is known as putting together and the craftsman is therefore known as a 'scissor putter-togetherer'.

Court 18, Garden street, late 1970s. Typically, workshops were built among houses and, since the needs of cutlers were few, many small workshops could be crammed into the yards and alleys almost anywhere. Such premises were more usual than the large factories of Rodgers and Wostenholm.

Doris Walsh, acid etcher, 1980s. Originally, the name of the knife manufacturer was struck on the blade using a mark punch. In the nineteenth century acid etching sometimes replaced this. The process requires that the trademark is copied on tissue paper, which is then pressed onto the blade. The inked pattern determines the area for the resist. Acid is then applied which eats into the exposed areas of the blade and creates the mark.

George Wostenholm, cutlery manufacturers. During World War II, many cutlery manufacturers were required to do 'war work'. This photograph shows fly presses being used to cut and shape

the items which were assembled at the bench. Because it was wartime there were more women employed than was usual.

Long-serving employees of Joseph Rodgers, 1911. In its published history, *Under Five Sovereigns*, the firm acknowledges the debt it owed to the skill, expertise and loyalty of such men. Note that cutlers wore white aprons. In the eighteenth century, journeymen cutlers were called 'apron men'.

After the Second World War, Eric Wragg, penknife cutler, worked for Wm Morton, cutlery manufacturers on Rockingham Street, and acted as caretaker for their premises. Here is a works' outing in the 1940s, probably to the east coast, with the coach firm Hirst and Sweeting of Holme Lane, Sheffield. Mrs Morton is in the centre of the back row, with the large hat.

Right: An engraving from an early twentieth-century catalogue of the Washington Works. George Wostenholm, cutlery manufacturer, built his business on the American trade and their name was linked with the legendary Bowie knife. They made all types of sporting knives, as well as razors, table knives and tradesmen's knives. Their trademark was 'I-XL' (I excel). In the foreground is a wall-mounted, hand powered crane by a first floor doorway. This was the despatch room, where wooden cases of cutlery could be lowered to waiting railway drays. The crane was still in use in 1972, when the factory closed.

Below: The derelict Washington Works shortly before demolition in the 1970s.

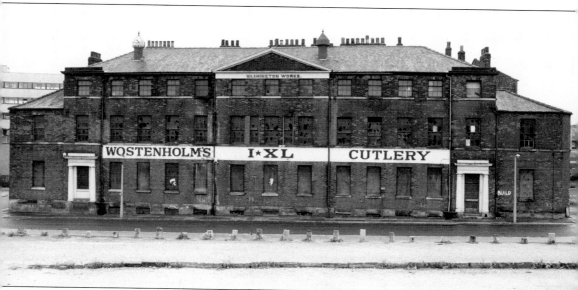

Derelict cutlery workshops, West Street, 1995. On the right of the top floor had worked a table knife cutler, George Sadler, and on the left, Eric Wragg and his wife, spring knife cutlers. On the floor below was Davidson, mark maker. The ground floor was occupied by Morton's shop, which sold cutlery. In the past, a cutlery shop in Sheffield was rare – most people knew someone in the trade who could get goods at a fraction of shop prices.

Richards Brothers, cutlery manufacturers, had one of the most modern cutlery factories in Sheffield, built on Moore Street after the Second World War. By using relatively unskilled labour – mostly women – to assemble precision-made parts, which did not require filing or fitting, the firm could produce a cost-effective product for the mass market. The 'LAMP POST' trade mark was commonly seen on souvenir knives and scissors bought at seaside resorts, where they would be displayed in a fan-shape on cards in shop windows. The firm no longer exists and the factory was demolished in the 1970s. The site is now a DIY store.

Swann-Morton, surgical blade manufacturers, Bradfield Road, late 1930s. Swann-Morton were originally manufacturers of 'wafer' blades – razor blades of the type introduced by Gillette. Several wafer blade manufacturers turned to making surgical blades, made by a similar process. The firm is one of Sheffield's twentieth-century success stories, having expanded greatly from this, their 1935 factory. As of 1999, the firm produces approximately five million surgical and industrial blades per week.

Swann-Morton's present factory on nearby Owlerton Green. The firm is one of the world leaders in this industry.

A Thomas Ward and Sons Ltd exhibition stand, 1930s, possibly at the British Industries Fair at Castle Bromwich, Birmingham. Not only was this a display of its goods, but there were many

examples of 'point of sale' ideas.

The first showroom of Joseph Rodgers, cutlery manufacturer, 1906. This, the most prestigious showroom in Sheffield, was at No.6 Norfolk Street. It was visited by both English and foreign royalty. The celebrated Norfolk Knife, a large spring knife with seventy-five blades, which was made for the 1851 Great Exhibition, can be seen at the end of the room on the right. Rodgers had an enviable reputation for quality and were considered to be the world's leading cutlers.

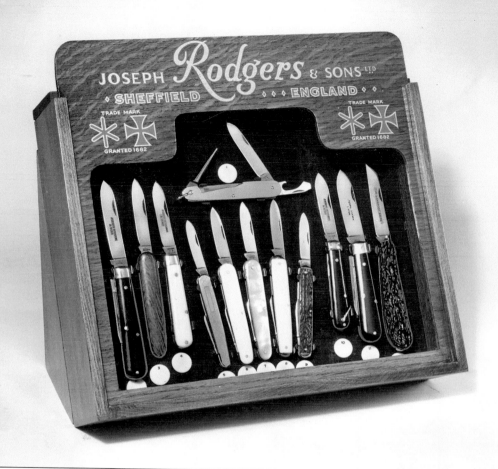

A post-Second World War counter display case for Joseph Rodgers folding knives. The case shows the variety of handle materials – the scales – which were used. Examples here are of horn, wood, pearl, stag, ivory and decorated metal. Technically, knives with a blade at each end were called penknives and those with two blades at one end were called pocket knives.

The Year Knife, made by Joseph Rodgers in 1821, was bought by Stanley Tools at auction in 1969 so that it would remain in Sheffield as an example of Sheffield skills and craftsmanship. Here, Walter Scales is preparing to add the blade celebrating the Queen's Silver Jubilee in 1977.

T.H. Stansfield, Garden Street, 1970s. Two men double hand forging mark punches. Punches were cut and filed with the design of the manufacturer, which was then stamped onto knife blades, etc.

Punch Forgers was formed in 1920 to produce steel blanks for the markmaking trade. This newly established workshop had a Blacker hammer as its main forging machine. These were used by many small manufacturers who had traditionally had a forger and striker for the heavier classes of work. The machine did away with the striker, thus keeping down the costs.

Basil Walker, markmaker, 1993. Sheffield cutlers from the sixteenth century marked their knives by striking an identifying mark into the blade. These marks were registered by the Cutlers' Company. The mark punch was made from steel, with the design cut and filed into the top. Basil Walker was one of the few remaining hand markmakers, the trade being taken over by machine-made punches and dies. This view of Basil's workshop shows the clutter, so typical of small workshops. The wonder is that Basil could find anything.

Two

Edge Tools

Light and heavy edge tools must have been made in Sheffield long before there is any firm documentary evidence. The best documented are the filesmiths, who joined the Cutlers' Company in 1682. Files were vital to many industries until the mass production of parts was sufficiently accurate that last-minute filing to fit was not required. Until then, myriads of different and specific files and rasps were made. The same processes of forging and grinding as in cutlery manufacture occurred in the file trade. The ground file blanks were then cut, originally by hand, with a chisel and hammers ranging in weight from a few ounces to several pounds. Many saw files were hand-cut by women in their own homes. Machine filecutting was introduced in the mid-nineteenth century.

The photographs in this section follow the processes of manufacture – forging, grinding, assembling and warehousing. In the early twentieth century many trade catalogues proudly carried photographs of processes and some have been used here – principally from the 1911 Ward and Payne catalogue. Manufacturers, however, are wary of showing too much of their operations to potential competitors and recent photographs have been more difficult to find.

The trades covered in this section are light and heavy edge tools, hammer manufacture, file, saw, auger and gimlet making. One interesting group of photographs is those covering the exhibitions and displays of tools at Trade Fairs. The change in promotional material over time is very evident.

John Bedford & Sons Ltd, steel and file manufacturers, *c.* 1900. On the right of the works yard is the crucible steel melting shop with its high, wide chimney – really a bank of chimneys set in a row. The roof 'lights' are shutters which let out the heat. The low building on the left is

probably a file forging shop. Note the escaping steam from the hammers. The works yard on a wet day is full of sludge and puddles, piles of used crucibles and coke and ash.

John Bedford & Sons, *c.* 1900. This view shows the Lancashire boiler, providing power for the

grinding shop and forges. The wheels in the foreground were for file grinding.

Mawhood Brothers, Trippett Lane, 1940s. Mawhood Brothers must have been one of the few smaller light edge tool firms casting their own steel. It is likely that their move in 1939 from Pond Hill to their new factory on Trippett Lane was dictated by an existing crucible steel furnace adjacent to the building plot. Here the 'puller-out' is seen preparing to lift the white-hot crucible and its contents from the furnace below his feet and place it on the floor for the teemer. The size of the crucibles can be seen from the stack of new ones on the shelves.

Clay Wheels Forge, 1890s. This water-powered 'nose' helve was the heaviest type of hammer and was used for 'cogging' steel ingots into blooms. This was the initial forging process after casting, performed in order to squeeze the steel and close the pores, making the ingot sound. The steel would then be rolled into bars of varying sections which became the raw material for the tool and cutlery trades.

Stanley Gregory, in 1985, demonstrating hand forging techniques at Wortley Top Forge, a seventeenth-century, water-powered iron forge. He is demonstrating welding a steel face on to an iron back for drawing out into a cutting tool. Many tools and cutlery have a keen cutting edge and, for economic reasons, were made from two or more pieces of metal. The expensive crucible-cast steel used for the cutting edge was too expensive for the main body of the tool, so common steel or an iron back was welded onto the cast-steel face. Examples of tools made in this way are heavy wood chisels, plane irons, sickles, scythes and carving knives.

Hallamshire Sheet Rolling Mills, 1960s. The sheet rolling trade provided the raw material for many local industries. The shovel, saw, hacksaw blade and cutlery trades all used sheet steel. Here, hacksaw blade sheet is being rolled, usually three sheets at a time. The roller stands ready to put the sheets through the rolls. The 'backer' catches the sheets as they come through and then passes them back over the top of the rolls. This process continues, reducing the sheets as required.

Thomas Firth, c.1910. File manufacture was one of the staple trades of Sheffield from at least the seventeenth century. After around 1870 many file firms began to use machines for forging and cutting. Pattinson, Forrest and other local engineers made these specialised machines for forging tools and cutlery. A skilled forger could make these machines 'talk'. Today, very few such machines are still at work.

Thomas Firth, *c.* 1910. File grinding was done to prepare the file blanks prior to cutting the teeth. The blanks were laid in rows on the bed of the machine, which then passed under the grinding wheel, making the rough blanks smooth. Subsequently, the other side and the edges were ground. Local industry provided these machines; Walters and Dobson of Bailey Street were for many years makers of machinery for the file and cutlery trades.

A filecutter's workshop, Langsett Road, *c.*1975. Before machinery was introduced in about 1860, little capital was needed to set up in one of the file-making processes, which could be carried out in lean-to buildings in gardens and courtyards. Possibly up to six filecutters would work here, sitting at stiddies facing the typical long run of windows. The file blanks were carried by the cutter from the manufacturer, with the cut files being returned on the next journey.

Hand filecutting. The leather stirrup held the file blank securely on the iron stiddy, mounted on a stone stock. The weight of the hammer could range from 7lb to 3-4oz. The triangular chisel, which cut the teeth, varied in width from half an inch to about three inches depending on the size of the file being cut. One of the last hand filecutters was Jack Brown of Creswick Street who finished work in the 1950s. He stayed in business making 'specials' – files which were uneconomical to cut by machine.

Machine filecutting at Thomas Turner, c. 1902. Cutting the smaller files, by hand and machine, was considered to be 'women's work'. The work was so noisy that speech was impossible in machine filecutting shops and, as in the textile trades, a form of lip-reading was developed. Machine filecutting was introduced to Sheffield in the 1860s and the last file manufacturing firm – Ralston of Rockingham Street, Sheffield – closed down in 1985. 'I can buy foreign files, finished, cheaper than I can buy the steel to make them,' said Jack Ralston.

Thomas Firth, *c.* 1910. File hardening at the turn of the century was considered to be an awful job. There were hardening furnaces, salt baths, lead baths and noxious fumes – all providing a very poor working environment. However, the quality of the file was largely attributable to correct hardening. The file hardeners' skills were stretched to the limit when dealing with half-round files. If the red-hot files were straight when quenched, because of their cross-section the files would come out shaped like a banana. To counter this, the files were bent before they were quenched and so became straight again.

Thomas Firth, *c.* 1910. The finished files were proved (tested for hardness), oiled and wrapped, usually in oiled brown paper, before being packed six or twelve to a box. The box would be labelled on the top with the company's name and on the end with a size label, giving the section, cut and size of the files – e.g. flat, smooth, 8 inch. The boxes were very heavy, being equivalent to a solid block of steel. In spite of this, much warehouse work was done by women.

F.G. Pearson's fork forge, 1910s. By modern Health and Safety standards this would be condemned as a death trap, with the uneven and untidy brick floor and unguarded belt drives. However, accidents were fewer than might be imagined, even with so many young boys 'learning the trade'. The Pattinson Brothers spring hammers were made in Sheffield and were used here to draw out the tines of forks. Coke forks had as many as twenty tines, each drawn out from a single piece of steel. The handle straps were usually welded on afterwards.

Ward and Payne, 1911. This gives a good idea of the layout of a heavy edge tool forge – the brick hearths for heating the tools being made, the steam hammers and the close proximity of everything. There is an air of efficiency here. The forger on the left is welding the straps on coke forks. The man on the right is stamping the 'set' in shovel plates. This work did not require a second man as hammer driver. Note the pile of shovel plates on the left.

F.G. Pearson, wood handle turning shop, 1910s. Most factories had more than one storey, with the forgers, grinders and hardeners on the ground floor. The upper floors had lighter work. Here, on the top floor, wooden handles are being produced. The woman on the left is French-polishing wooden chisel handles with a rag while the man is turning a handle on a lathe. In the foreground is a pile of fork handles.

F.G. Pearson's, fork warehouse, 1910s, showing hay forks ready for dispatch. This was no doubt a seasonal trade, with high stocks just before haymaking time. The digging forks, with straps right up to the D-shaped handle, were known as Best Steel Strong Agricultural Forks. Typically, the young lady is wearing a brown paper apron.

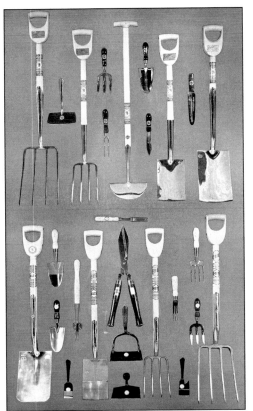

A selection of stainless-steel garden tools from the 1930s history of CT Skelton of Heeley. At this time stainless steel was a new material for garden tools. Because the blades were mirror polished, they were much easier to use, since the soil did not stick to them. However, the high production costs meant that only gentlemen gardeners could afford them.

CT Skelton of Heeley was one of the largest manufacturers of shovels, spades and forks. Here, a 1930s shipment of shovels, etc. is starting its journey to South America. This shipment gives an idea of the vast quantities of goods manufactured in Sheffield and exported all over the world. Many older Sheffield residents can remember these enormous Scammell lorries of the heavy haulage firm Attercliffe Engineers Transport Ltd.

Mawhood Brothers, Trippett Lane, 1940s. This small edge tool firm moved in 1939 from Pond Hill and built new premises. The offices were on the first floor, the grinding shop on the ground floor and the furnaces, with the crucible stack, on the left. The yard was at a lower level than the front building. The caretaker's house can be seen at the end with the 'boss's' car in the garage. The windows to the right were for the warehouse.

Mawhood Brothers, 1940s. The men on the left and right are smithing, or cold straightening, gouges, a process carried out after hardening and tempering. In the background is a gas-fired furnace, possibly for hardening the tools.

A light edge tool grinding shop at F.G. Pearson, 1910s. Here a variety of tools would be ground – wood chisels, plane irons, etc. Notice how each man is in a different position as they perform different tasks. The man in the centre has his blade under a 'flatstick' while the man in the background uses the 'robin' to help him grind thin scrapers. The dust extraction pipes hang from the ceiling, useless at that distance from the grinding wheels.

Stanley Tools, Ecclesfield factory, 1960s. Wood chisels are being placed in a rotary grinding machine. Traditionally, all edge tools and cutlery had been hand-ground by skilled grinders. After the Second World War, fewer men were prepared to do the heavier grinding and manufacturers were forced to mechanise many processes with machines such as this.

F.G. Pearson's light edge tool warehouse, 1910s. A variety of tools can be seen here waiting to be finished and packed – augers, spokeshaves, turnscrews (screwdrivers), hand forks and joiners' bevels. Wrapping paper hangs from the ceiling and it appears that the handles of rows of turnscrews have recently been polished and laid out to dry. The pulley was part of the lift system for raising and lowering goods to and from the floor below.

William Marples' catalogue of 1909 has photographs of many of its production processes. This is the spokeshave workshop. Spokeshaves were usually made from beech, although boxwood and ebony were also used. Wood is stored on the left with sacks ready for the sawdust and waste wood. Because of their complex shape, spokeshave making was always a hand trade, with little machinery being used. The last spokeshave maker, Cyril Smith, retired in the 1960s.

Albert Victor Bock making planes at William Marples, 1960s. Traditionally, many wood planes were made in London, Birmingham, York, Bristol and elsewhere, but 95% of the plane irons, the cutters, were made in Sheffield. After 1900, demand decreased and Marples decided to make their own planes, with craftsmen coming in from the other cities. Albert was the last planemaker to make handmade bench planes at the Hibernia Works, Sheffield, and retired in 1966. He originated from Birmingham, where he learned his trade.

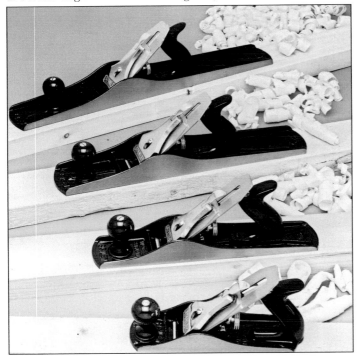

Joiners' planes have been made in Sheffield for almost 200 years, the earliest being made of beechwood. By the 1930s, however, metal planes were being produced, with at least six Sheffield planemaking firms involved in the trade. These are Stanley metal bench planes used for planing wood. Wood from sawmills may not be straight or flat. The long plane at the top is used to take off the 'hills' without going into the 'hollows'. Smaller work requires the use of shorter planes – the most commonly used being the 9-inch smooth plane, shown at the bottom. Many other patterns of plane are made.

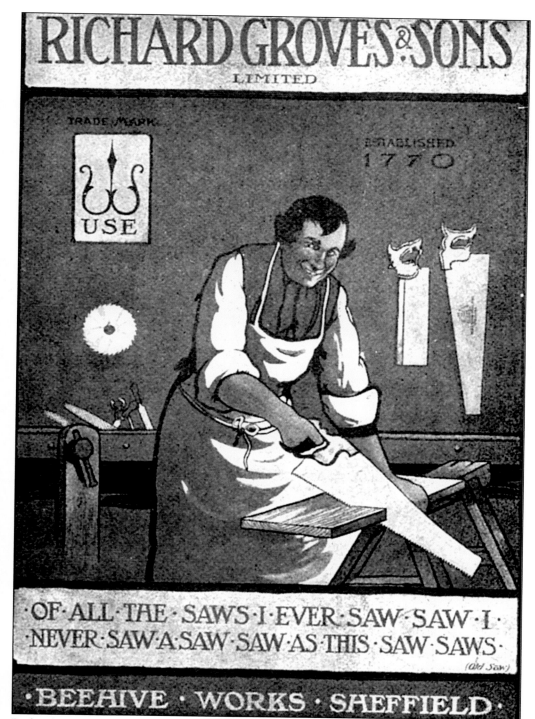

Richard Groves, sawmakers. This illustration is from a 1915 Groves catalogue. The old 'saw' still provides amusement as people try to make sense of it. The trademark is typical of the late eighteenth century when the firm began.

WK & C Peace, Mowbray Street, 1930s. Circular saw hardening was a heavy, dirty and smelly job. The heated blade was dropped into a tank of whale oil, which was used as a quenching medium because it did not ignite even at relatively high temperatures. Improvements in oil technology produced a substitute, which removed one reason for killing whales.

Herbert Buttery, hand saw setter, Spear and Jackson, 1950s. The saw trade has been practised in Sheffield for at least 250 years, requiring a tremendous amount of expertise to produce high quality saws. Saws were traditionally made from hot-rolled sheet steel, which had to be flattened with a hammer and anvil – a skilled trade called smithing, one of several hand processes. When cold-rolled steel strip was introduced many of the earlier difficulties in manufacture disappeared. Machines took over handwork and the world of sawmaking was taken over by engineers. Here, Herbert sets the saw by knocking the teeth alternately left and right, so that the saw will not bind in the cut.

Sanderson Brothers and Newbould hand saw department, 1970s. The man is handfiling saw teeth. Later, only the 'Best' quality saws were set and sharpened by hand. Many years of practice ensured that both setting and sharpening were achieved at lightning speed, because men were on piecework. The piecework rate until around the 1970s was based on a 'Statement' dating back to 1844.

Sanderson Brothers and Newbould. Here, tenon saw backs are being set, while the handsaw plates are being 'viewed' – undergoing their final inspection.

Sanderson Brothers and Newbould. In the handsaw department in the 1970s, women are wiping and wrapping back saws. In the background is Brian Marsh, the saw department manager, who served his time at another sawmaking firm – Francis Wood of Henry Street, Sheffield.

Ward and Payne, 1911. Sheep shear manufacture was a major Sheffield trade, with twenty-one firms listed in the 1898 trade directory. Ward and Payne pioneered the manufacture of shears blanked out from steel sheet instead of being made from iron 'tagged', i.e. forged, with a shear-steel edge.

Ward and Payne, 1911. Grinding sheep shears was a specialist job. The grinders were in a union and disputes sometimes resulted in strike action.

Ward and Payne, 1911. Sheep shear bending was, and is, the most highly skilled job in the trade. Today, one firm, Burgon and Ball, Sheffield, still make sheep shears and have only one or two benders. Attempts were made to automate this process but failed, as the automated process was not fast enough!

Ward and Payne, 1911. Most warehouses looked like this: quiet havens in an otherwise noisy factory. Each parcel would contain six sheep shears. The paper was cut, folded and wrapped immaculately – a work of art. The parcels would then go to the packing room to be placed in wooden cases for shipment.

Trade Union Sheep Shear Company, 1920s. Their works were at Oughtibridge, to the north of Sheffield. In the late nineteenth century, in a trade dispute with manufacturers, the union members walked out. They contacted the Australian Sheep Shearers Union, who agreed to use only Trade Union Sheep Shears, produced by the union men, who set up their own works.

During the 1970s, there was much industrial unrest in the country. Footprint Tools suffered a strike from June 1973 to January 1974.

Footprint Tools made their own dies for stamping and for drop hammers. The dies were cut on a milling machine. This die was for stamping hedge shears.

Thos R. Ellin, Footprint Works, 1968. This firm has been for many years a manufacturer of metal-cutting shears. Here a two-ton drop stamp forges the blades.

John Ridge, gimlet forger, Ecclesfield, late 1960s. John Ridge was the last of a long line of gimlet hand forgers in Ecclesfield. He was eighty-four years old and still working after seventy-five years in the trade. Shortly after this photograph was taken, the local authority pulled down the smithy and a garage was built on the site. As was typical of 1960s redevelopment, little regard was given for the historical value of the workshop, processes and tools.

Footprint Works. From the mid-nineteenth century, much forging in the cutlery and light edge tool trades was performed by goff or spring hammers. These machines ran very fast and the one seen here is forging solid-centre auger bits.

Auger twisting at Thos. R. Ellin, Footprint Works, Hollis Croft, 1968. A red-hot rod of steel, with the end previously flattened, is given a twist on this machine. Two jaws in the centre stop the blank turning, while the crank handle on the left rotates the hot end into a twist.

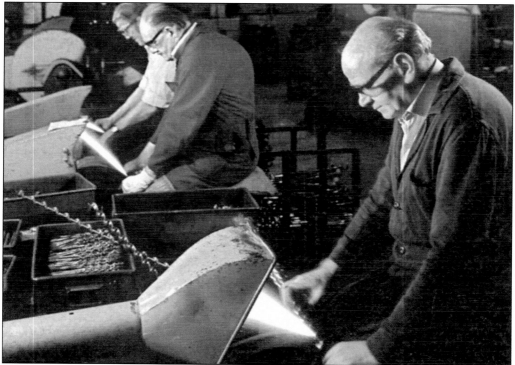

Record Ridgway, 1970s. Grinding twist augers looks an easy job, but it required great skill in taking off just the right amount of metal.

F.G. Pearson, 1910s. This is the heavy edge tool warehouse. The augers are marked either with Pearson's name or that of another firm for whom they were making augers. The bench doubles as a row of cupboards, possibly for keeping stock in.

Tyzack Sons and Turner, 1957. This is a posed photograph of the scythe tilt. The workman is shown holding the blade as if plating, i.e. flattening the blade to the right width, but he is using the wrong hammer! The left-hand hammer is always used for forge welding and drawing out the 'skelp' – the part-made scythe. The right-hand hammer is for plating.

Thomas Staniforth's Hackenthorpe works, 1930s. Staniforth were long established as makers of scythes, sickles and agricultural tools. The worker is smithing flat a 'Little Giant' grass hook blade prior to grinding. Strimmers have taken over from garden tools such as this.

Stanley Works (GB) Ltd. In 1958, Stanley built a new factory at Ecclesfield about five miles north of Sheffield. It was designed to produce hammers and wood chisels. Here, John Shaw uses the drop stamp to forge hammer heads. In the mid-1990s, hammer production ceased and by the late 1990s production was relocated to the Hellaby Works, east of Sheffield.

Stanley Works (GB) Ltd, Ecclesfield, 1968. A close-up of forging claw hammer heads. With three blows of the drop stamp the hammer head is formed on the end of the red hot bar. The work was hot, noisy and dirty. In order to keep production going, three men worked as a team – one as the furnaceman, one forging the hammer heads and the third resting after forging. Each man rotated to the next job at 20-minute intervals.

Stanley Works (GB) Ltd. Stanley became famous for making joiners' claw hammers. They were a firm favourite with most woodworkers, being well designed and beautifully balanced. After forging, the hammer heads were hardened, tempered and then shot blasted. Dick Crossley watches them tumbling from the conveyors into storage bins ready for grinding.

Stanley Works (GB) Ltd, 1960s. Hilda Hardy is putting the hammer heads on shafts using a hydraulic press. In destruction testing on the hammer head, it took one and half tons pressure to pull the head off the handle. In the late 1990s many hammers have steel shafts, covered with rubber grips. Although the designs of the handles vary, none seems to feel as nice as a good wooden shaft.

Stanley Works (GB) Ltd, 1960s. Grinding off protruding edges after the shaft has been fitted to the hammer head.

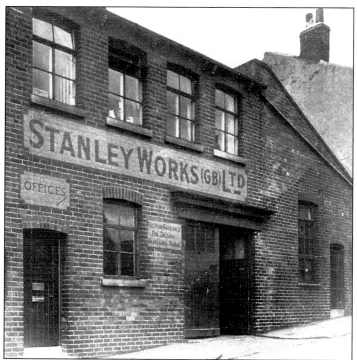

In 1936 Stanley Works of the USA gained a foothold in Sheffield's tool manufacturing industry by buying the firm of J.A. Chapman Ltd, who made joiners' braces and planes, hand drills, etc. This is a view of the front entrance and office. It seems a far cry from the firm's present-day factory site.

Stanley Works (GB) Ltd, 1960s. This is the front of the new factory of Stanley Works (later Stanley Tools) at Ecclesfield. The plant was originally used for the production of hammers and wood chisels, although other products were made here from time to time.

An aerial view of the Parkway works of Record Tools Ltd, built in the 1960s. The original works and offices are in the foreground and the Disamatic automated foundry is the building with the smoking chimney. Behind the original building is the extension for the automated vice production and warehouse. The firm celebrated its centenary in 1998.

Record Tools Ltd invested heavily in a new automated foundry at the Parkway Works for making the castings which would form the basis of vices, cramps, pipe tools, etc. In this view the metal is being poured into moulds, which are on a continuous conveyor belt.

J. & R. Dodge. This Sheffield firm exported tools around the world. This is their trade stand at the Amsterdam exhibition of the 1890s. Saws and machine knives were among the many products supplied by the company.

G. Roberts, cabinet makers, made this exhibition stand for Turner, Naylor & Co. at the 1907 London Exhibition. Similar showcases full of tools were destroyed when Turner, Naylor and Co. closed in the 1960s. This photograph came from Billy Hukin, Sheffield's last razor grinder. It was given to him by his father-in-law, G. Roberts.

C. & J. Hampton's trade stand at the British Industries Fair at Castle Bromwich, Birmingham, 1930. The main products on show are vices, Stillson pattern wrenches and other pipe tools. It was not until 1931 that the firm began making planes.

K.W. Hawley (Tools) Ltd, Earl Street, c.1980. This was a display of old tools to attract interest. The tools now form part of the Hawley Tool Collection housed at Sheffield University.

Stanley Works (GB) Ltd. This trade stand was at Bridlington in the 1960s, where an educational crafts conference was being held. Stanley were very aware that if students were introduced to their tools from the beginning, they probably had a customer for life.

Firth Tools, *c.* 1910. Many Sheffield cutlery and tool companies displayed their products in showcases at exhibitions. Small items such as knives, twist drills, etc. could be displayed in pleasing arrangements. This is a display of engineers' cutting tools – an important part of Sheffield's industries.

As a final note on Sheffield tool manufacture, this picture shows a joiners' toolmaking shop on the top floor of the building at F.G. Pearson in the 1910s. Joiners' tools included bevels, squares, spokeshaves and, strangely, ice-skates, which were included because of their similar methods of manufacture. Note the stacks of wood. The condition of the floor was not unusual in Sheffield workshops. The walls needed a new coat of whitewash – 'bug blinding' as it was known in Sheffield.

Three

Silver

The manufacture of sterling silver and silver-plated items involves more manufacturing processes than cutlery, largely because of the decorative nature of the objects. Handmade items are still being produced, alongside the mass production using presses. The basic processes involve the shaping of flat sheets of silver or nickel. Originally this was done by hand, by hammering on 'stakes' or anvils. The improved quality of dies in the late eighteenth century, following the invention of the crucible steel process, meant that mass production could be introduced. Steel dies could make an article and press the decoration into it at the same time.

Having shaped the article, or parts of it, the teapot or candlestick was then assembled, with the parts being soldered together by the silversmith. Decoration, either by chasing, piercing or engraving, could then be applied.

The final stage was buffing and polishing. Buffing flatware was traditionally done by women, while most hollow-ware was buffed by men. Buffing was a filthy job. The articles were buffed on revolving cloth wheels, using a mild abrasive of oil and sand. The change from dull metal to the polished sparkling silver is stunning.

Silver and plated items were 'luxuries' and the range of decoration and styles was enormous. As well as the mass-produced flatware, the spoons and forks, the silver manufacturers produced teapots, sugar bowls, jugs, trays and candlesticks, which are termed 'hollow-ware'. Some of the Sheffield silver firms were huge, building very large factories. Firms like James Dixon, William Hutton, Mappin and Webb and Walker and Hall employed hundreds of people. They all had prestige works and their showrooms were tourist attractions. Sadly, not one of these giants survives.

Heeley Silver Rolling Mills, early twentieth century. The firm produced blanks in non-ferrous material, mostly nickel silver, for the flatware and hollow-ware trades. Cast nickel-silver ingots were rolled into sheet and blanks then cut out, which were sold to other manufacturers as the

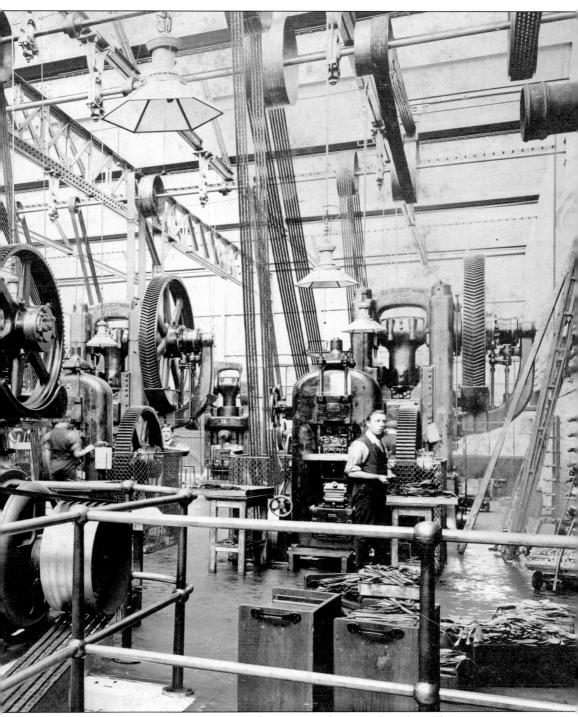

raw material to make into their finished products. Here, the several modern Bliss presses were probably used for blanking out tea trays, teapot bodies, etc. In the foreground are spoon blanks.

This most unusual press at James Dixon and Sons, Cornish Place, c.1900, was used for blanking out spoons and forks. It had its own steam engine to drive it – most other machines were driven by leather belts and line shafts transmitting power from a single, large beam engine.

Mappin and Webb, 1920s. This is the spoon and fork department where they are 'cross rolling' spoon blanks. In this process, the spoon blank is passed between the ends of two steel rolls. This made the blank thinner and wider so that the spoon could then be 'bowled'. The work is being done by girls – small in contrast to their machines.

Mappin and Webbs, 1920s. This delightful picture typifies the Sheffield cutlery trade of that era. Cross rolling spoon blanks was a dirty, monotonous job feeding countless blanks through the ends of rolls With such potentially dangerous machinery, it wouldn't do to lose concentration!

Mappin and Webb, 1930s. Mr Kenny is working at a drop stamp. The falling weight, or 'tup', is at the top centre. The process here is 'bowling' spoon blanks. The blank is carefully positioned on the bottom die and when he pulls the handle, the tup falls. This process went on with great rapidity. Unfortunately it appears that one time Mr Kenny was too quick with the drop stamp or too slow in moving his fingers. The first finger of his left hand is missing.

A spoon and fork buffer, James Dixon and Sons, 1930s. Notice how she picks up five spoons at a time in her right hand, while her left hand has picked up a handful of Trent sand and oil mixture, which she then feeds on to the spoons. The abrasive does the work, the wheel being the vehicle for this to happen.

This massive fly press at James Dixon, *c.*1900, must predate the friction presses used for deep-drawing hollow-ware and producing trays, etc. The flywheel effect is used to produce the necessary downward thrust.

Press shop at Mappin and Webb, 1922. Here deep bowls and bases for cake stands are being made. Thousands of such items were produced for the catering trade, for cruise liners, railway dining cars and hotels. This trade has all but disappeared with changes in travel and eating habits.

The manufacture of silver-plated articles for hotels, railways and shipping lines required mass-production processes. This is the battery of heavy hollow-ware stamps at Mappin and Webb in 1922. The stamp beds were set into deep pits which, before vibration-absorbing mats existed, were filled with leather parings and offcuts. The stamp block was lowered onto this and allowed to settle. There was sufficient 'give' in this, even after many years, whereas if the block had been set solidly on concrete, the vibration might well have damaged the machinery.

Mappin and Webb's plating shop, 1920s. Electroplate came into use in the 1840s and replaced Sheffield plate. The tanks held a solution into which articles were suspended. The electric current passing through the solution caused silver to be deposited on the surface of the articles.

When the duckboards underfoot were worn out, they were sent to sweep smelters where special furnaces were able to recover any silver that had been spilt in solution.

Mappin and Webb, 1950s. Miss Saltfleet, acid etcher, is placing a paper transfer on a bowl. The transfer carried the pattern and, after a process of applying a 'resist' to parts of the design, acid would eat away at exposed areas. This was quicker and cheaper than engraving a design.

Mappin and Webb, 1920s. Finishing off silver or plated hollow-ware. The enormous amount here suggests that it is one large order, perhaps for a steamship. It appears that rigorous checks were being made to ensure every piece was perfect. Such an order today would be rare, occurring perhaps when a cruise ship was being commissioned.

Wallace Smyth, designer, Mappin and Webb, 1940s. After leaving the Sheffield School of Art in 1926, Wallace Smyth joined Mappin and Webb and rose to be head of the design studio, retiring when the firm closed in the early 1960s. Here he is (centre) showing the chain of office for Haltemprice UDC, together with the design. The design and execution were considered to be a work of art and the chain was therefore exempt from purchase tax.

A series of photographs showing various manufacturing processes were taken at Atkin Brothers in 1939. Casting molten metal, either silver or nickel silver, was the beginning. The metal is being cast into an ingot mould and when cold, the ingot will be rolled into sheet form. The process is similar in many ways to casting crucible steel.

The rolling mill was introduced in the Sheffield area for the iron trade in around 1665. The same process was used for rolling silver and Sheffield Plate into sheet material around 1740. At Atkin Brothers these rolled sheets were the raw material from which most silver articles were made.

An Atkin Brothers die-sinker cuts by hand the steel dies for stamping the intricate, decorative parts of a piece, which were then soldered on to the main body. This was highly skilled and artistic work. It was never seen by the customer, but the dies were a valuable and very important part of the stock of a silver manufacturer.

Atkin Brothers. Stamping is a method of producing decorative mounts and mouldings which are later soldered to the edge of an article. By using dies in a drop stamp, the decorative effects can be produced in sizeable quantities and quite cheaply. The alternative would be 'chasing' by hand, but the cost would be prohibitive.

A close view of the process of spinning a dish at Atkin Brothers. In the background are some of the many wooden 'chucks', or 'formers', used for spinning silver bowls, etc.

Metal spinning is the process of forming ductile sheet metal over a former or chuck. This was done on a lathe with long-handled spinning tools, which gently push the rotating metal against the wooden chuck. It was a process which produced round hollow-ware, such as cake dishes, teapots, and so on. The article would be made up of different parts soldered together. This workshop was at Walker and Hall in around the 1920s.

Silversmiths at Mappin and Webb, around the 1930s. Left to right: Messrs Howard, Fisher, Chapman, Vessey, Norton and Barker. Silversmiths were craftsmen who might 'handraise' a

bowl or teapot, or would assemble parts.

Mappin and Webb, 1920s. The silversmith is assembling parts of a coffee-pot. Because of the octagonal shape, the body, foot and lid would have been stamped out, rather than spun or handraised. Here, he is soldering the knob onto the lid. His left hand holds the solder in a pair of tongs and the gas/air blowpipe is in his right hand.

Atkin Brothers, 1939. The process of soldering a mount – a decorative edge – on to the sheet silver is called 'mounting'. The loose mounts are held in place with iron wire clips shaped like a closed letter 'C'. These grip the two pieces together while heat and solder are applied.

Atkin Brothers, 1939. Buffing is the initial polishing process which starts to give the silver its lustre. It is commonly supposed that all buffers were women, but they did the lighter articles such as spoons and forks. Heavier work was always done by men. Both types of buffing are very dirty and arduous and few people today are prepared to do this sort of work. However, it is an essential part of the manufacturing process and must be done correctly.

Mappin and Webb, 1930s. Saw-piercing is like fretwork, creating designs by cutting away the metal. A paper pattern is glued onto the bowl or tray and small holes drilled where the metal is to be cut away. The piercer threads a very fine saw blade through the hole and reattaches it to the saw frame. The shape is then cut out and the process repeated dozens of times until all the shapes are removed. The precision and care needed is immense – mistakes cannot be corrected.

Atkin Brothers, 1939. Hammering gives the body of a dish its final contours. The pack hammer is an adaptation of a planishing hammer, with a face of saw plate wired to the head and leather or cardboard sandwiched between the head and the wired plate. This gives softer, kinder blows to the metal and avoids stretching the silver.

Mappin and Webb, 1951. Mr Joe Barker chasing a shield that was to be attached to a bowl commissioned by the British Allied Manufacturers Association for the endowment of a Chair of Electrical Engineering at Cambridge University. Because the silver has no colour, various lines and patterns were used to represent the colour as described by the College of Heralds. The designer, Wallace Smyth, had to work closely with the chaser because of the complexity of the work.

Mappin and Webb produced many silver gilt Lonsdale Belts until they proved too expensive. Wallace Smyth, designer at Mappin and Webb, made cardboard templates in eight weight categories, ensuring the belts would always fit.

Mappin and Webb, 1930s. Mr Norton, a chaser, is working on a Lonsdale Belt. Chasing is the art of making a design in relief. The design is drawn on the article and a tool similar to a small, fine chisel is held vertically above the line and tapped with a small hammer. By moving the tool, a fine groove is formed and the pattern produced. The silver being worked is held steady on a bed of pitch.

Atkin Brothers, 1939. Engraving is one of the last processes in decorating silver. Engraving is the cutting of a series of fine lines on the surface of the silver using small hand-held gravers. These tools are about 3-4in long with a mushroom-shaped handle – small enough to be held in the palm of the hand. Here, at Atkin Brothers, Harry Kugler is engraving the veins of a vine leaf.

Atkin Brothers, 1939. The final finishing processes are similar to buffing – giving the surface of the metal a smoother texture. This was followed by burnishing, which was usually done by women. Burnishing tools had long, straight handles with a variety of agate and hardened steel ends. These were rubbed over the surface of the silver to give it its final gleam.

A finished Atkin Brothers vine dish. The production processes have included rolling the silver sheet, stamping the mounts, spinning the dish and foot, hammering the contours, soldering the mounts and base, saw-piercing the pattern, engraving the decoration, buffing and polishing. Such amounts of handwork are now infrequent.

A Second World War air raid shelter at James Dixon and Sons, Cornish Place, one of many cellars in the factory. This was possibly a practice air raid. Notice the different style of dress – the trilbies and flat caps of the men, while the women had turbans. Perhaps one can differentiate between the office staff and the craftsmen.

Heeley Silver Rolling Mills during the First World War. As in the cutlery trade, silver manufacturers were directed to war work during both World Wars. Here, the deep drawing

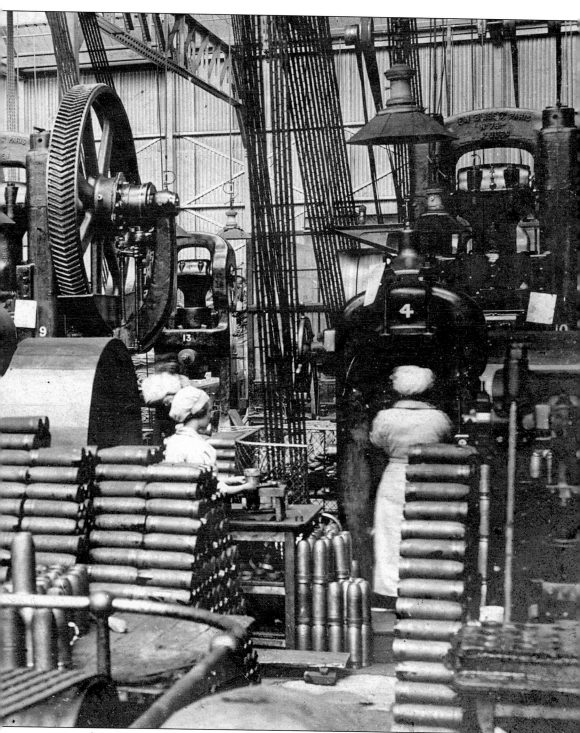

presses are making brass cases for shells.

This is the staff of a small silversmith firm called A Beardshaw in 1919. Their works were at 32

Victoria Street. The group is typical of many small firms, with an interesting mix of ages and sexes.

In July 1906 James Dixon and Sons celebrated their 100th anniversary. Twenty-two tram cars took the 1,200 employees and guests from here at Penistone Road to Firth Park and then by 'brakes' to Shire House at Ecclesfield, home of one of the Dixons. On the top deck of the leading car was the band of the 1st Hallamshire Rifles.

The James Dixon and Sons centenary luncheon at Shire House, Ecclesfield, July, 1906. The large marquee was for lunch and tea, speeches and presentations.

The following three photographs are examples of commissioned pieces from Mappin and Webb and illustrate the diversity of craftsmanship and manufacture. In 1904 Mappin and Webb produced a bedroom suite for the Raj Rama Bhawaur Singh in India. This is the bed – 8ft long by 6ft wide by 13ft high. There were also fourteen chairs, four tables and two large dressing tables.

This is a 1/10th-scale model in sterling silver of a Morris Minor 1000. It was crafted by Mappin and Webb in 1957 for Viscount Nuffield, GBE, FRS, DCI, on his seventieth birthday. As there were no works drawings for the car, the designer Wallace Smyth had to visit the local car showroom of Kennings to measure up a real one.

Mappin and Webb produced this piece of regimental silver for the officers of the 38 Corps Engineering Regiment, who served on Christmas Island in 1958. Christmas Island was the site of hydrogen bomb tests in the 1950s.

Glossary

bloom	an ingot after the initial forging process
buffing	a polishing process using a rotary linen mop dressed with a fine abrasive
chasing	raising decoration on the surface using punches
crucible steel	high-quality homogeneous steel used in the manufacture of scissors, spring knife blades and many cutting tools
engraving	incised decoration using sharp scribing tools
etching	using acid and resist to produce surface decoration
forging	hammering heated steel into the shape of a blade or component
grinding	using an abrasive wheel to put a sharp edge on a blade and make it smooth
horsin/saddle	the seat in a grinding trow
ingot	solidified steel after it has been cast or poured into its mould
parser	a drill rotated using a fiddle bow to bore a hole
penknife	usually a small spring knife with blades at both ends
pocket knife	usually a larger spring knife with blades at one end only
pressing	a metal forming process using a fixed-stroke ram
putting together	joining the two parts of a pair of scissors
raising	the gradual hammering of flat sheets into a hollow shape
saw setting	the alternate bending sideways of saw teeth, which prevents the saw binding as it cuts
saw-piercing	fretwork designs made by sawing into bowls, etc.
scales	the two flat pieces riveted to form handles of knives, razors, pocket knives
setting in	attaching an open razor blade into the scales (handle)
smithing	the striking of a blade with a hammer to correct any errors in flatness
spinning	forming flat, ductile sheet onto a mould rotating in a lathe
spring knife	a folding knife with one or more blades working on a spring
stamping	a metal forming process using a free-fall weight
stiddy	an anvil
stock	a wooden or stone stand for an anvil
trow	the grinding wheels, water trough and seat, collectively